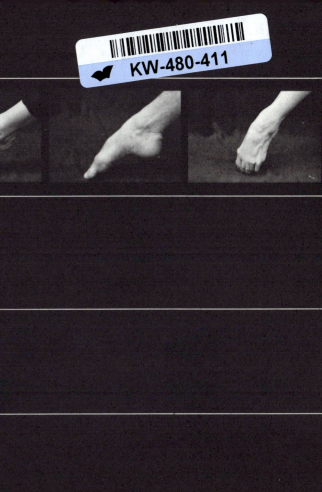

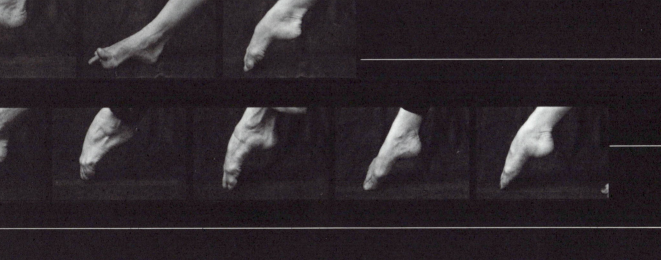

THE COMPANY WE KEEP

THE COMPANY WE KEEP

by

Wayne Eagling, Robert Jude and Ross MacGibbon

ANGUS & ROBERTSON PUBLISHERS

All the photographs in this book were taken by the authors.

ANGUS & ROBERTSON PUBLISHERS

London   Sydney   Melbourne   Singapore   Manila

First published in the United Kingdom by
Angus & Robertson (UK) Ltd in 1981

First published in Australia by
Angus & Robertson Publishers in 1981

Copyright © 1981 by Wayne Eagling, Robert Jude
and Ross MacGibbon

ISBN 0 207 95950 1

Typeset in 10pt Eras Book by Showbill Typesetting, Sydney

Book design by Michele Withers and Neil Carlyle

Printed in Hong Kong

CONTENTS

INTRODUCTION

The Royal Ballet as we know it evolved during the 1920s and is, essentially, the product of two remarkable and distinguished women: Ninette de Valois and Lilian Baylis. Ninette de Valois had been a member of Diaghilev's stunning and exotic Ballet Russes and, after leaving Diaghilev's company, founded the Academy of Choreographic Art in London in 1926. That same year she met Lilian Baylis who was manager of the Old Vic theatre, famous for its Shakespearian plays and opera. Together, they hoped to re-open a second theatre — Sadlers Wells — as a base for both opera and ballet, and a home for Ninette de Valois' group of dancers.

By 1931 they had achieved their aim, and the Vic-Wells Ballet and School, as it was then called, had its permanent address in Rosebery Avenue. It gave its first performance on 5 May 1931, with Anton Dolin as a guest. To start with, the new ballet company performed at both theatres but eventually it was decided to stage only plays at the Old Vic, and opera and ballet exclusively at Sadlers Wells. Just re-built, Sadlers Wells must have looked bright and attractive then. Now, fifty years later, the Sadlers Wells Royal Ballet is trying to raise £3 to £4 million to improve the stage conditions.

One of the most important requirements for the young company was to have a repertoire of classical ballets such as **Swan Lake**, **Giselle**, **Coppélia** and **Casse Noisette**. Fortunately this was made possible with the stagings of Nicholas Sergueyev, the former régisseur of the Imperial Ballet in St Petersburg, and with the participation of the great classical dancers Alicia Markova and Anton Dolin. Over the next eight years the company continued to grow and improve. In 1933 two renowned guest artists appeared with the ballet — Lydia Lopokova dancing the part of Swanilda in **Coppélia**, and Stanislas Idzikowski as Harlequin in **Carnaval**; and in 1934 Alicia Markova and Anton Dolin appeared in **Giselle**. Ballet stars such as these began to attract large and enthusiastic audiences and helped to put it in the public eye. Markova was, in fact, a regular member of the company, and also appeared in **Casse Noisette** and **Swan Lake** in 1934.

The company also proved itself in other ways, especially in the fostering of young talent. In the 1934 production of **Swan Lake**, for example, Alicia Markova was partnered by a young Australian and, in the same year, a young ballerina had her first solo role in the de Valois ballet of **The Haunted Ballroom**. Both are now household names: the Australian was Robert Helpmann and the ballerina was Margot Fonteyn.

It was not only the dancers, however, who were to make the company so renowned. Constant Lambert, the musical director and conductor, made an enormous contribution to its success as did Frederick Ashton with his superb choreography. Many other names associated with the company in its early days are now legends of the theatre themselves — the costume designer Cecil Beaton, the painters Edward Burra and Rex Whistler, designers like Sophie Fedovitch, William Chappell and Hedley Briggs and composers like Arthur Bliss, Gordon Jacob and Gavin Gordon. All of these people gave a special magic to the company's performances and stagecraft and their involvement with the ballet demonstrates the extent to which the company was in touch with current theatrical trends and artistic thought during the 1930s (although it always kept a balance between traditional and modern productions).

With the outbreak of war in 1939, the London theatres had to close. Sadlers Wells itself became a rest centre for bombed-out families. The company, now homeless, went on tour with a rigorous and demanding repertoire of full-length classics and one-act ballets. Various members, including Michael Somes, William Chappell and Alan Carter, left to join the forces. The remainder spent most of the war years travelling from town to town and theatre to theatre, in constant peril from air raids and faced with an inadequate diet and all the shortages and discomforts of the time. On one memorable occasion a British Council tour in the Netherlands happened to coincide with Hitler's invasion of the country. Narrowly avoiding capture, the company escaped to safety but lost, in the process, all its costumes, scenery and orchestral scores.

Yet, despite the difficulties and despite having to cope with extra performances (sometimes there were as many as three on one Saturday alone) the company prospered and thrived, and its members exhibited an unflagging vitality and zeal even during the worst moments of the war. Robert Helpmann, in particular, emerged as both a first-rate performer and an excellent choreographer. His ballets such as **Hamlet** (revived by the Royal Ballet in 1981) and **Miracle in the Gorbals** were vivid and compelling theatrical experiences, sometimes inviting controversy, and they attracted a completely new audience to the art of ballet.

At the end of the war the company joined ENSA in full and went abroad to perform in Germany and the newly-liberated countries. On their return, they mounted a season at Sadlers Wells.

Then came a quite unexpected and thrilling invitation – to become Covent Garden's resident ballet company. It was a marvellous opportunity and Ninette de Valois did not hesitate to accept. On 20 February 1946 the Royal Opera House curtain rose for the first time on a sumptuous and opulent production of **The Sleeping Beauty** featuring, once more, the sparkling talents of Margot Fonteyn, Robert Helpmann and Constant Lambert.

The parent theatre in Rosebery Avenue was not neglected. A new company was formed, called the Sadlers Wells Theatre Ballet, comprised of students, senior members of the main company and some young dancers from the commonwealth, including Nadia Nerina and Alexander Grant. It was a nursery for some notable talent, and ballerinas and principal dancers often moved from there to the main company. Among these new stars were David Blair, Nadia Nerina and Donald Macleary. The Theatre Ballet created new works and was a testing ground for the inspired ideas of bright young choreographers such as John Cranko and, later, Kenneth MacMillan.

In the meantime the main company was experimenting with the potential presented by the large Covent Garden stage and in 1946 Ashton's superb **Symphonic Variations** was performed. Leonide Massine staged, and performed in, the revivals of **Boutique Fantasque** and **Tricorne** and in 1948 Ashton's magnificent **Cinderella** helped to reverse the trend in favour of one-act ballets rather than full-length productions. The company also made an historic visit to the USA in 1949, opening in grand style at the Metropolitan Opera House on Broadway, New York, and thereafter made frequent trips across the Atlantic. Later on, the company also exchanged visits with Russia and performed in France.

During the 1950s, though, it was the lively second company that was to herald new and refreshing ideas. Rising choreographers like Kenneth MacMillan and young dancers brought a youthful vigour, appeal and excitement to the stage. In 1958 MacMillan's ballets **The Burrow** and **Solitaire** won critical acclaim while **The Invitation**, two years later, was greeted with a mixture of rapture and outrage. Its overtly sexual theme was an early harbinger of the 'permissive society' and marked a new era in ballet.

In 1956 the now world-famous Sadlers Wells Ballet was granted a Royal Charter and the two companies became known as the Royal Ballet. Then, in 1963, Frederick Ashton succeeded Ninette de Valois as artistic director.

During the 1960s a new generation of principals came to maturity, including David Wall and Doreen Wells, who were different but just as enthralling to watch as their predecessors of the 1930s, '40s and '50s. The glittering partnership of Antoinette Sibley and Anthony Dowell emerged; Merle Park was hailed as a prima ballerina and Lynn Seymour shone as an inimitable actress/dancer. And Margot Fonteyn's performances with Rudolf Nureyev brought wildly appreciative applause. The choreographers likewise introduced fresh themes; Ashton created the lovely **Monotones** and **Enigma Variations** while MacMillan produced **Romeo and Juliet**.

In 1970 MacMillan became director of the company after Ashton's retirement. It was also decided, that year, to re-organise the touring company and make it smaller and more experimental. It was re-named the New Group but, unfortunately, the venture failed and thus the company returned to its original policy of staging classics, some twentieth-century revivals and some contemporary works. It also went back to its old base at Sadlers Wells theatre and had another change of name — this time to the Sadlers Wells Royal Ballet. The move proved invigorating and the second company has produced some particularly talented new choreographers.

Throughout the 1970s the Royal Ballet relied mainly on a repertoire of ballets created by overseas choreographers like Balanchine, Robbins and Cranko although they also premiered ballets by outsiders — such as Glen Tetley's **Field Figures** and Rudi van Dantzig's **Ropes of Time**. There were some revivals as well but, aside from Ashton's **A Month in the Country**, it was largely MacMillan who was responsible for creating new works. **Manon** and **Mayerling** (1978) are probably his most popular and successful ballets of recent years.

MacMillan retired as artistic director in 1977 to become principal choreographer. He was succeeded by Norman Morrice, an ex-director of the Ballet Rambert, who has followed a policy of allowing young dancers to test their abilities in main roles instead of inviting guest artists.

Today, there is another new and eager generation at the Royal Ballet. Among its rising stars are dancers like Stephen Jefferies, Wayne Eagling and Lesley Collier whose performances show the meticulous attention to detail, fine training and artistic flair which have become the hallmark of the company. Plus, of course, that extra little something that makes the Royal Ballet so special.

In 1981 the Royal Ballet celebrated its fiftieth birthday. We are all looking forward to another fifty years as brilliant and exciting as these last have been.

Dame Ninette de Valois

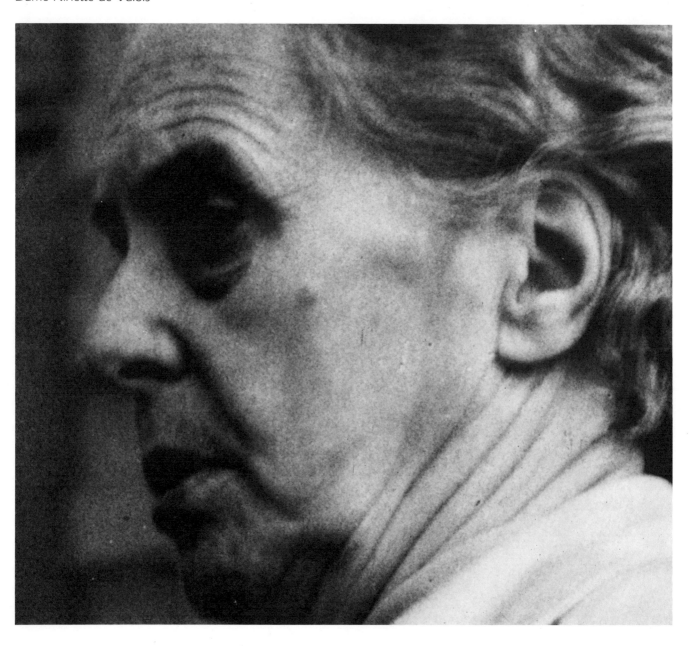

Sir Fred takes a curtain call (on stage for his 70th birthday celebrations)

A gallant kiss for Dame Margot (a gala performance to commemorate her 60th birthday)

A flock of seasoned professionals.
Joyce Wells (Ladies Wardrobe, retired),
Alexander Grant (Director, National
Ballet of Canada),
Kenneth MacMillan (Principal
Choreographer, Royal Ballet),
Gerd Larsen (Principal Teacher),
Leslie Edwards (Director, Royal Ballet
Choreographic Group),
Michael Somes (Répétiteur),
Henry Legerton (Régisseur),
and kneeling — Jill Gregory (Ballet
Mistress),
Brian Shaw (Principal Teacher);
the survivors of the first American tour,
celebrating the 25th anniversary of the
company's triumphant début in New
York.

A lion amongst the cubs—Michael Somes and members of the _corps_

"Like this?" Graham Fletcher receiving guidance from Dame Ninette

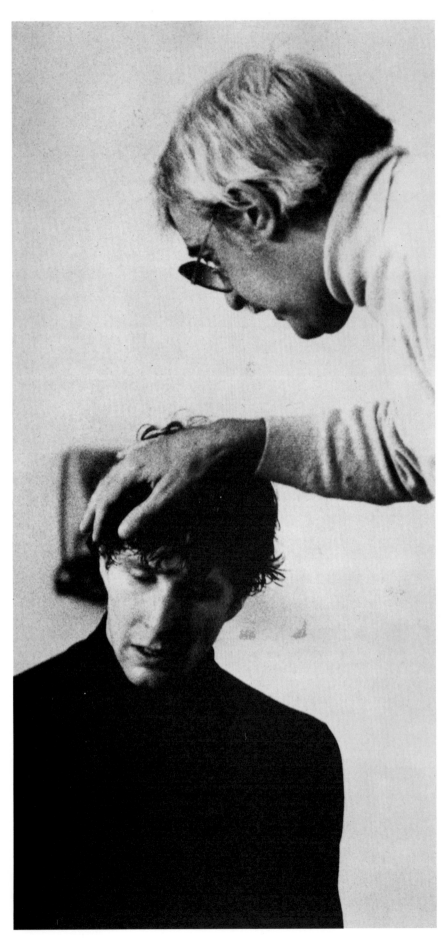

A comforting hand
for Wayne Eagling
from Kenneth MacMillan

"Of course you can dance in them" — Gerd Larsen reassures Anthony Dowell before Swan Lake

Wall to Wall—
David Wall and his
wife Alfreda Thoroughgood

"Girls don't make
passes at guys who
wear glasses."

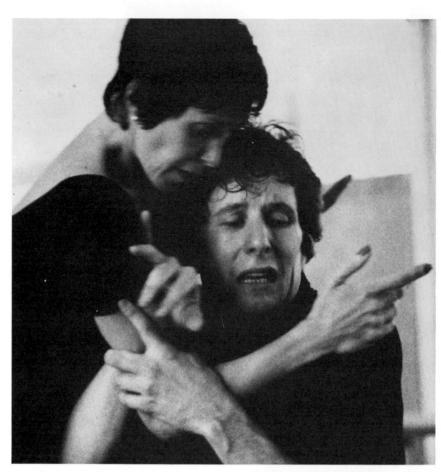

A studio rehearsal of _Mayerling_, featuring Wayne Eagling as Prince Rudolf and Alfreda Thoroughgood as Countess Larisch. Although they have performed this ballet many times, constant rehearsal is essential as both may perform the same roles with different partners for different performances and may well be performing in a different ballet on the same day. To add to the complexity, in this particular ballet Alfreda dances in two different roles

Left: Comfort and advice from Sir Fred for Marguerite Porter

Right: "Well in my day . . ." Jill Gregory and Gerd Larsen watch from the side of a rehearsal room

Left: Mirror image? No-Wendy Ellis and Alfreda Thoroughgood

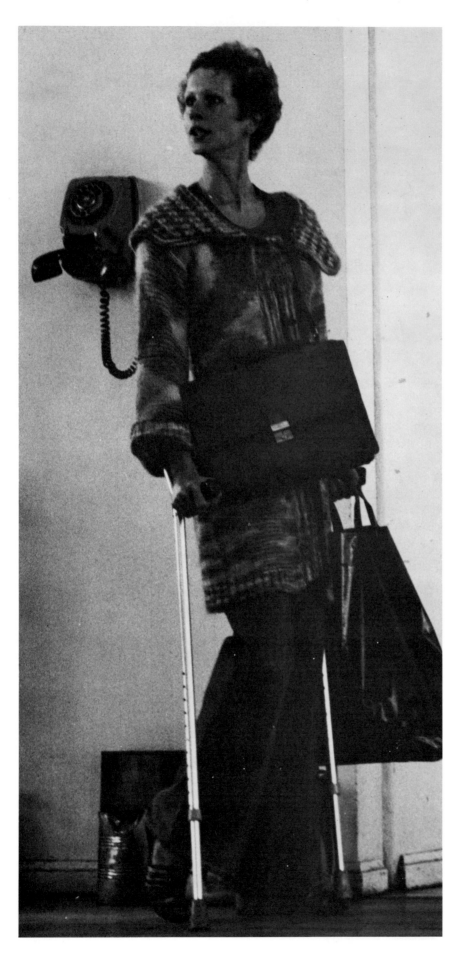

"I don't think I'll be able to manage the fouettés tonight." Ballet dancing is not always the glamorous life one imagines — Jenny Penney on crutches after spraining her ankle in rehearsal

It often feels as if most of the time is taken up sitting around waiting for something to happen—
Lesley Collier,
Jennifer Penney

Derek Rencher and Monica Mason

Top: Wendy Ellis   Bottom: Brian Shaw and Wayne Sleep

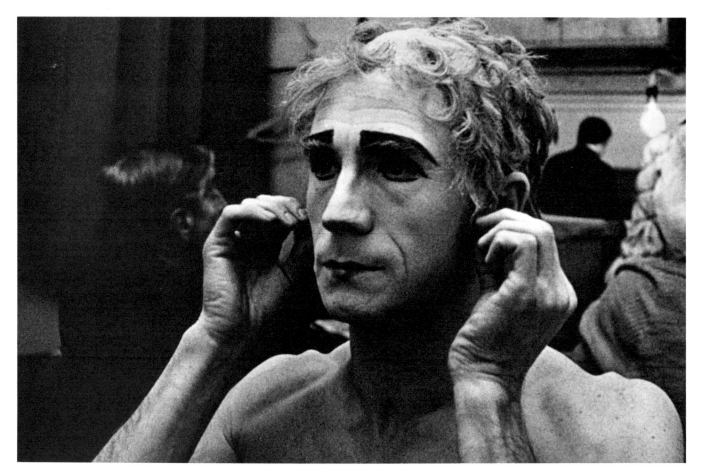

Top: Michael (Bunty) Coleman   Bottom: Norman Morrice (Director, Royal Ballet)

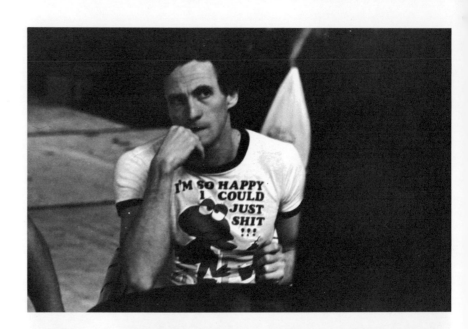

The many moods of
'Bunty' Coleman. Mike
entered dancing
relatively late in life
(seventeen) after
having first tried his
hand as a photographer's
assistant.

Lesley Collier, on the other hand, started dancing at the age of two when she enrolled at a local ballet school.

Iris Law (Artistic Administrator) shares a private joke with Anthony Dowell

Ross MacGibbon

Ross MacGibbon and Robert Jude

Marguerite Porter, Wayne Eagling and Robert Jude

Mark Silver

Pippa Wylde

Anthony Conway

33

Top (Left to right): Sharon McGorian, Jane Devine and Gail Taphouse
Bottom (Left to right): Joanna Allnatt, Laura Connor, Mark Silver and Genesia Rosato

Top: Vergie Derman and Julian Hosking.　　Bottom: Party spirits!

Wayne Sleep.

Crush Barre — Every dancer's day starts with class, whatever the situation and wherever the location. The morning class warms up the muscles of the body, allows scope to work on aspects of technique and also serves to strengthen one's body

for the arduousness of the performance. The facilities at the Royal Opera House are such that the corps de ballet still have to do their morning class on the carpet in the Crush Bar, while the soloists and principals are packed into a tiny studio below the stage.

The precarious position of the
Grant (Arts Council). Garry Grant

Right: MEN AT WORK
Top: Brian Shaw taking class with
Andrew Ward, David Wall and Robert
Jude
Bottom: Robert Jude, Garry Grant and
Christopher Carr

A helping hand —
often many hours
go into practising a
movement which, on
stage, is performed
in seconds

Class on stage outside Theater Wolftrap, Washington D.C.

Rehearsal for **Mayerling**. Wayne Eagling and Lesley Collier

Flying high —
Laura Connor hoisted
aloft in a rehearsal
for _Mayerling_

Mercury rising —
Freddie Mercury
(pop star) is held aloft
in a rehearsal for a
charity gala in aid
of mentally
handicapped children

Change of pace –
Not the Kind of
movement you see
every day at Covent
Garden. Here everyone
is getting ready for a
gala where the mood
was definitely relaxed.
It was a relief to get
off the toes and into
the heels. Despite
Mick's tee-shirt, a
good time was had
by all.

Notes on stage – Sir Fred and cast

"See you after the show"

"These Russian defectors aren't all they're cracked up to be"

Backstage view

Mad moments –
Corps de ballet in _Les Biches_

Lesley Collier in _Manon_

Derek Rencher incensed

Waiting for the curtain— while the audience enjoys a quick drink in the Crush Bar the conductor, Robert Irving, sits patiently backstage with the dancers and crew who wait tensely for the third act of Swan Lake.

This is the moment when comments can be exchanged between those on stage and the conductor concerning the performance in the act just completed.

Getting it right —
in the orchestra stalls
Wayne Eagling and
Merle Park receive
instructions from
Sir Frederick Ashton
on the correct arm
positions for
Symphonic Variations

The same movement
in performance

Someone was missing from the rehearsal . . . but did turn up for the performance

*"...and pretty maids
all in a row"*

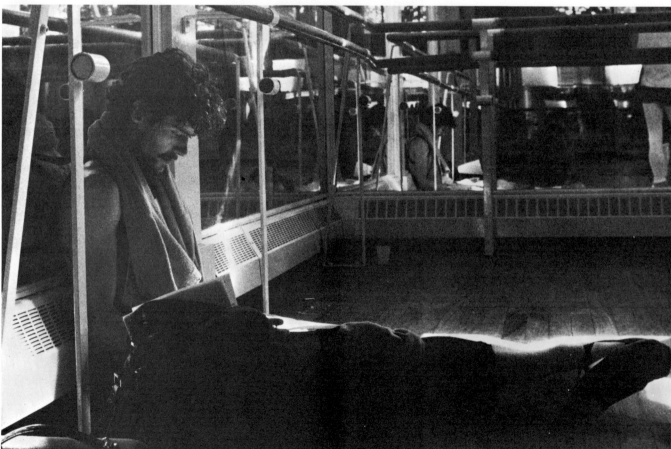

Three bars rest: David Wall and Stephen Jeffries (top), Mark Silver (below) and . . .

Antony Dowson with Sharon McGorian

It takes not only energy but also a lot of patience to be a ballet dancer

Sitting pretty

"You get all dressed up for the opening night and this is the best seat you can get!"

Lesley Collier

Top: Hilary Tickner   Bottom: Christine Woodward

Top: Rosemary Taylor, Jennifer Jackson
Bottom: Rosalyn Whitten

Jennifer Penney selects . . . and tests her shoes

Top: Waiting for the call   Bottom: Sew darn bored

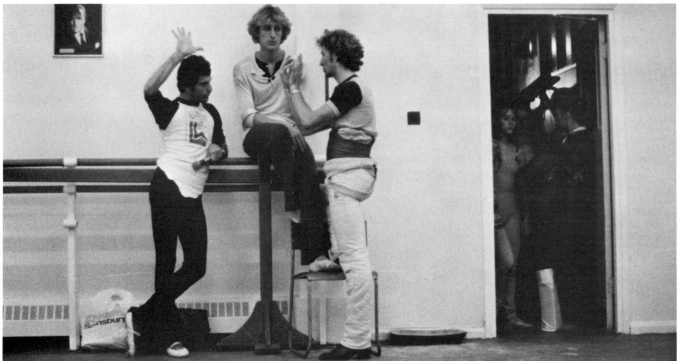

Top: Wayne gets a tip for the 3 o'clock at Epsom   Bottom: Wayne gives a technical tip to Freddie Mercury

Left to right: Wayne Eagling, Wayne Sleep, Derek Rencher and Mark Silver

Making up is hard to do—especially in cramped dressing rooms!

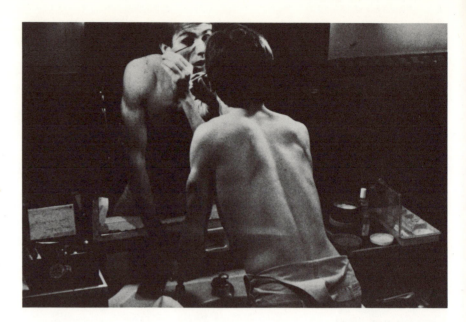

A little tea-cup reading?

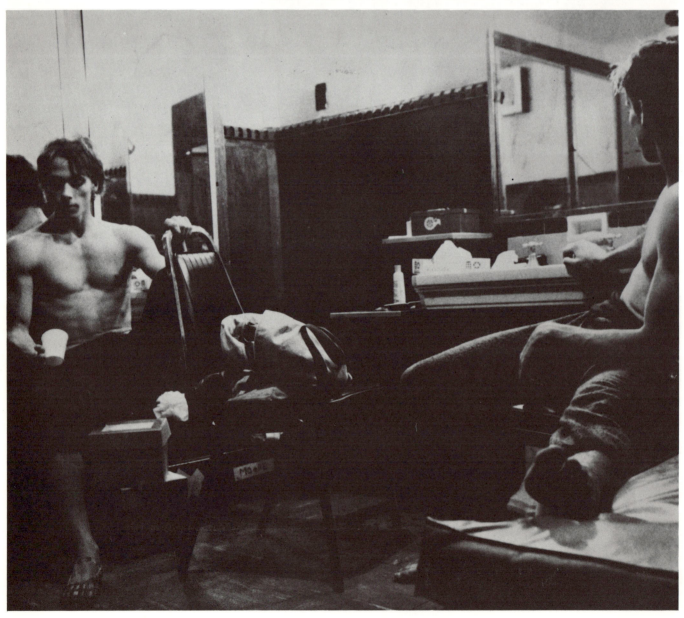

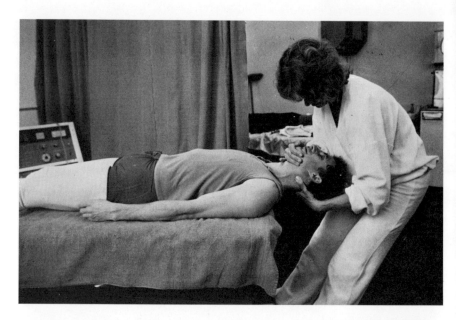

Body shop –
"Stretching a point"

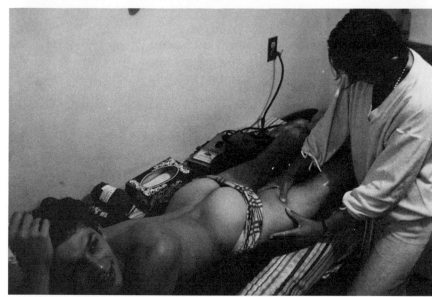

"Actually, it's my ankle..."

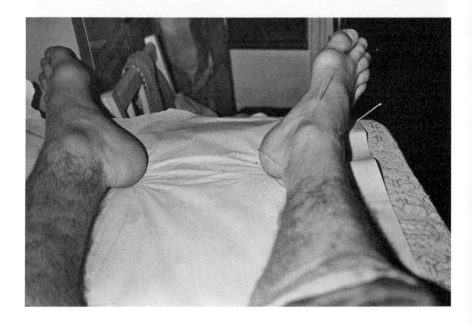

Acupuncture –
Definitely non-standard
at Covent Garden

A little help from your friends—Merle Park and husband

Monica Mason — a touring casualty

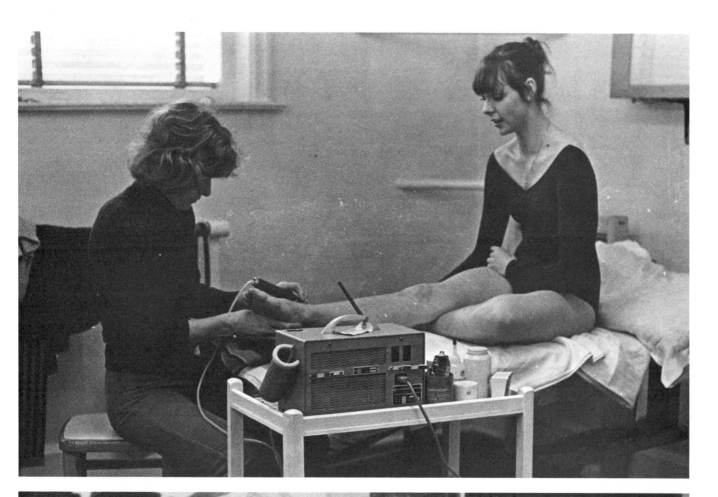

Top: Ultra sound—the standard treatment   Below: "What really gets my back up is that this is the third cast change this week."

Marguerite Porter
rehearsing Les Biches

75

Weary . . .

. . . but happy (Lesley Collier and Anthony Dowell)

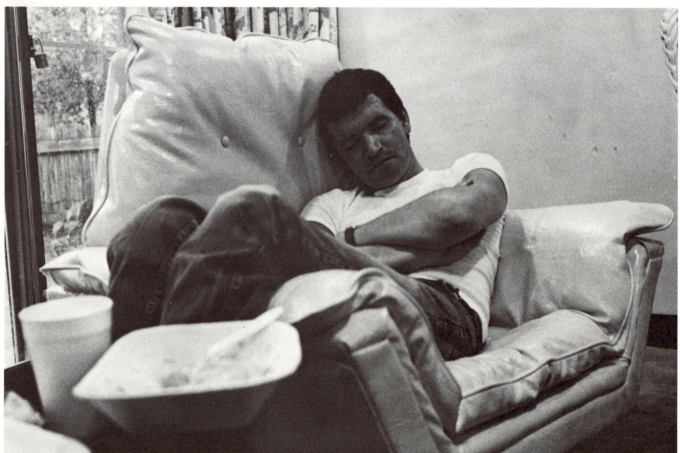

Top: On tour . . . but dead to the world   Bottom: Michael (Mother) Brown—Wardrobe Master

Ross and Ashley . . . sleeping beauties?

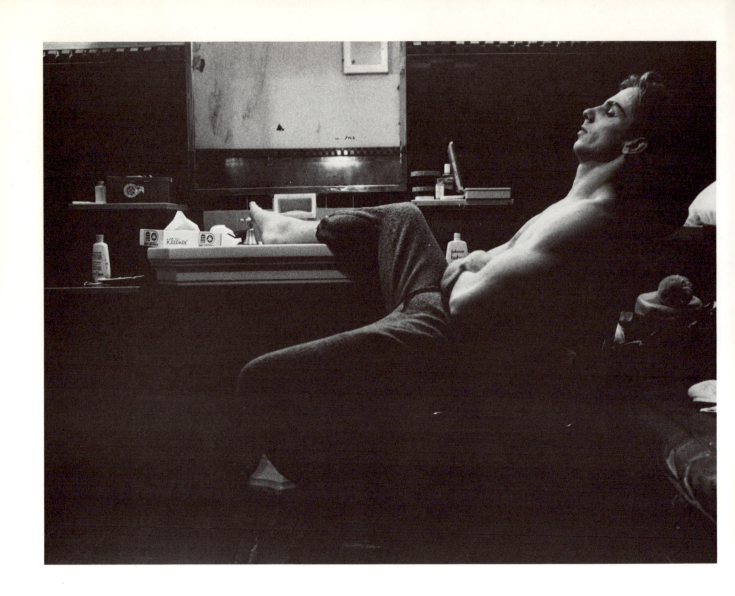

After classes all morning and performances at night, sometimes interspersed with a lot of travel... one becomes adept at sleeping almost anywhere

"On the road again"—
touring the world
with a ballet
company is not
always as glamorous
as you might imagine.
There are tons of
luggage to move,
hours of waiting
around in airport
lounges and then
the horror of
trying to get some
sleep on endless
flights. Still, it's
probably worth it all.

Extensions to Covent Garden being put to use ahead of schedule? Actually, no. It's the company working outdoors in Athens— not to packed houses it would seem. In fact the two figures who appear to have bought aisle seats to a less-than-sell-out performance are Paul Findlay and Norman Morrice. That's Ashley Lawrence rehearsing the orchestra.

Not a pretty face. Derek Rencher dressed (partly) as one of the ugly sisters

Top: Ex-classroom serving as dressing room   Bottom: But a little more rehearsal space than at home

*No, there's no-one
to do your
washing for you...*

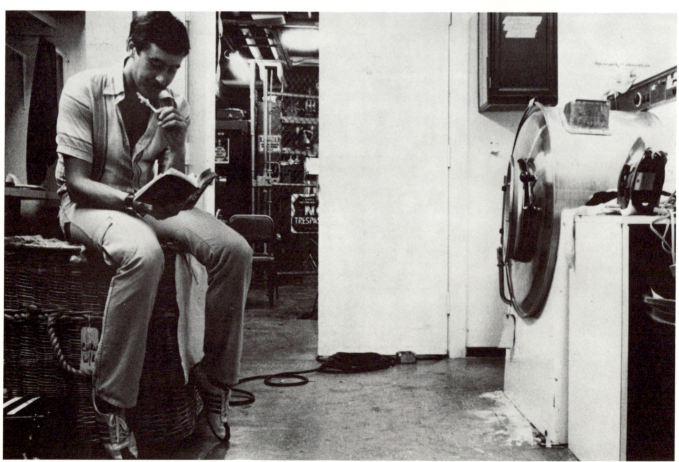

...which might
surprise these young
Korean autograph
hunters huddled
around a glamorous
star of the ballet
(Marguerite Porter).

There are many ways of relaxing between the endless round of classes, rehearsals and performances. We like to play cricket. That's Ross squatting for an important shot. Wayne is triumphant after a magnificent hit, whilst Robert is a somewhat distracted wicket-keeper.

Others prefer a less
strenuous form
of relaxation.

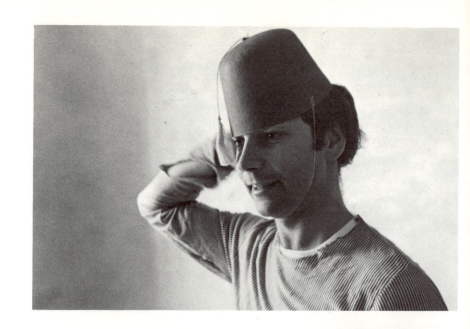

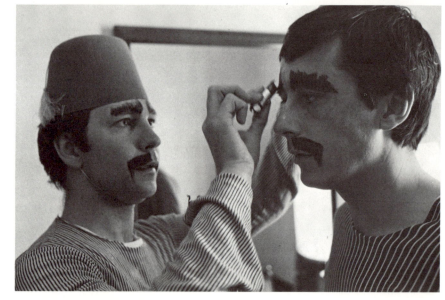

Some like to turn their hand to something a little more creative. The city is San Francisco, the characters are Paul Benson and Anthony Conway. The scene is a little amateur busking. The pictures tell the story.

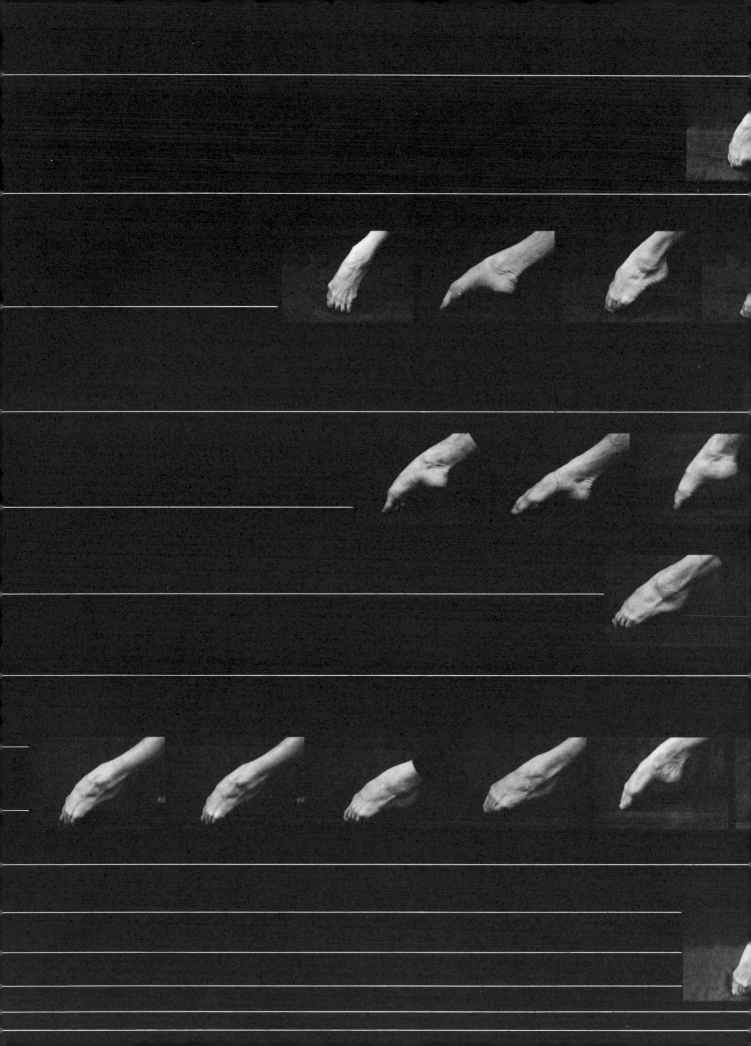